PRINCE AGHATOR IDUBOR

EDO CULTURE
IGODOMIGODO (HISTORY OF BENIN)

Copyright © 2023 by PRINCE AGHATOR IDUBOR

All rights reserved. No part of this publication may be reproduced, stored or transmitted in any form or by any means, electronic, mechanical, photocopying, recording, scanning, or otherwise without written permission from the publisher. It is illegal to copy this book, post it to a website, or distribute it by any other means without permission.

First edition

This book was professionally typeset on Reedsy.
Find out more at reedsy.com

Contents

BOOK DESCRIPTION	iv
ABOUT THE BOOK	v
IGODOMIGODO	1
THE BENIN PEOPLE	3
BENIN CULTURE	5
THE ROLE OF THE BENIN PEOPLE IN SHAPING THE BENIN CULTURE	7
THE BENIN LANGUAGE	9
NAMES OF OGISOS	11
LIST OF BENIN OBAS	13
BENIN TRADITIONAL RELIGION	15
HOLY ARUOSA (THE BENIN CHURCH)	17
THE BENIN TRADITIONAL FASHION	18
THE BENIN TRADITIONAL FOOD	20
BENIN ARTS AND CRAFTS	22
THE ROLE OF ARTS IN THE BENIN CULTURE	24
FESTIVALS AND CELEBRATIONS OF THE BENIN PEOPLE	26
THE TRADITIONAL MARRIAGE CEREMONY OF THE BENIN PEOPLE	28
THE TRADITIONAL BURIAL CEREMONY OF THE BENIN PEOPLE	30
SOME TOURIST SITES IN BENIN	32
SITE AND SOUNDS OF THE BENIN PEOPLE	34
CONCLUSION	36

BOOK DESCRIPTION

"EDO CULTURE: IGODOMIGODO (History of Benin)" is an interesting and thorough investigation of the rich cultural legacy of the West African Benin people.

Through this book, readers will learn about the unique customs, beliefs, and practices that have shaped the Benin culture for centuries.

From the traditional art and music of the Benin Kingdom to the religious and spiritual practices of the people, this book delves deep into the heart of Benin culture. It explores the role of the monarchy in Benin society, the importance of family and community, and the significant role that oral tradition plays in preserving the history and culture of the Benin people.

Filled with richly detailed descriptions, Anyone interested in the numerous and intricate cultures of West Africa must read "EDO CULTURE: IGODOMIGODO (History of Benin)."

Whether you are a student of African culture, a traveler planning a trip to Benin, or simply someone who loves learning about new cultures, this book is a valuable resource that offers a unique and in-depth look at the Benin culture and traditions.

ABOUT THE BOOK

"EDO CULTURE: IGODOMIGODO (History of Benin)" is a fascinating and educational book that gives a thorough account of the rich cultural heritage of the West African Benin people.

Written by an expert on African culture, this book offers a detailed look at the customs, beliefs, and practices that have shaped the Benin culture for centuries.

Throughout the book, readers will learn about the traditional art and music of the Benin Kingdom, the role of the monarchy in Benin society, and the importance of family and community in Benin culture.

The book also explores the significant role that oral tradition plays in preserving the history and culture of the Benin people, and includes beautiful illustrations that bring the Benin culture to life.

In addition to providing an in-depth look at the Benin culture and traditions, "EDO CULTURE: IGODOMIGODO (History of Benin)" also contains useful data, such as what to see and do, for tourists considering a vacation to Benin.

In general, "EDO CULTURE: IGODOMIGODO (History of Benin)" is a useful tool for anyone curious to learn more about the numerous and intricate civilizations of the BENIN PEOPLE. Whether you are a student, a traveler, or simply someone who loves learning about new cultures, this book is a must-read for anyone interested in the rich and fascinating culture of the Benin people.

IGODOMIGODO

Ogiso Igodo, the first Ogiso, gave the Benin kingdom the name Igodomigodo. IGODOMIGODO translates to "country made nation," "king made kings," "great men made nations," "great leaders build nations," "wisdom made wise men," or "great men made great nation," depending on the situation.

Igodo, an inspirational, youthful, intelligent Edionwere from the Idunmwun Ivbioto area, rose to become the Oka'iko.

In a coup, Igodo declared himself the Ogiso and abolished the Ik'edionwere. To help him establish his influence, he founded the Odibo-Ogiso group.

He implied that he was descended directly from Pa Idu, the eldest son of Osanobua (God) from the sky, by using the name Ogiso.

He designated Ugbekun as the seat of his expansive nation-state, which he called Igodomigodo. The inhabitants of Igodomigodo joyfully embraced Igodo as their leader. They regarded him as Pa Idu's reincarnation and gave him heavenly attributes.

They moved the God-son creation myth as well as all other myths connected to Pa Idu to Igodo. Naturally, all Ogisos and Obas of Benin work to support these myths in a number of ways, such as by refusing to eat in front of the people and therefore implying that they are capable of going without food. They are god-kings in myth, not mortal, and they are associated with a celestial mystery.

Igodo, the first ogiso (King), who formed the first dynasty of what would later be known as the Benin Empire (which reigned from roughly 1180 to 1897 in the region of the present-day Federal Republic of Nigeria), gave the kingdom the name Igodomigodo, according to Edo oral history (and not in the area of the unrelated, current Republic of Benin). Oba Eweka I altered the name of the kingdom from Igodomigodo to Edo, replacing the earlier ogiso era.

Eweka I, the first Oba, established the oba dynasty to replace the age of the ogiso (and child of Oranmiyan).

Since Eweka I changed the name of his empire to Edo, its inhabitants have been referred to as Edo people (or ovbi-do, "child[ren] of Edo"). The dynasty established by Igodo of Igodomigodo's first oba, Ewuare II, is currently headed by its 40th and 89th obas.

The kingdom of Igodomigodo was founded by Igodo, the first ogiso (king) in the area of present-day Nigeria. According to Edo oral history, this kingdom was the precursor to the Benin Empire, which existed from around 1180 until 1897.

The ogiso era was eventually replaced by the oba dynasty, which was founded by Eweka I, the first Oba and child of Oranmiyan. Eweka I renamed the kingdom Edo, and since then its people have been referred to as the Edo people or ovbi-ẹdo, meaning "children of Edo." The current Oba, Ewuare II, is the 40th Oba and the 89th ruler of the dynasty that was established by Igodo of Igodomigodo.

THE BENIN PEOPLE

The Benin people are an ethnic group located in West Africa, primarily in present-day Nigeria.

The history of the Benin people is long and complex, with evidence of human habitation in the region dating back to the Paleolithic Era.

The Kingdom of Benin, also known as the Edo Kingdom, was a pre-colonial African state located in what is now modern-day Nigeria.

The kingdom was founded in the 13th century and lasted until the late 19th century. The capital of the kingdom was the city of Benin, which is now known as Benin City.

The Kingdom of Benin was a highly organized and centralized state, with a strong bureaucracy and a powerful military.

The kingdom was known for its sophisticated artistic traditions, including bronze and ivory sculpture, as well as its highly developed system of trade and commerce.

The kingdom also had a complex system of social hierarchy, with a powerful royal family at the top and various classes of nobles and commoners below them.

In the late 19th century, the Kingdom of Benin came into conflict with European colonial powers, particularly the British Empire.

In 1897, the British launched a military expedition against the kingdom and captured Benin City, leading to the eventual colonization of the region.

After the fall of the Kingdom of Benin, the Benin people were subjected to colonial rule and various forms of exploitation. However, they also resisted and resisted colonial rule in various ways, including through armed resistance and non-violent protests.

After Nigeria gained independence from British colonial rule in 1960, the Benin people have continued to play a significant role in the country's political and cultural life.

Today, the Benin people are a diverse and vibrant community, with a rich history and a bright future.

Benin Culture

The Benin people of Edo state, located in Nigeria, have a rich and diverse culture that is deeply rooted in tradition and history.

The Benin kingdom, also known as the Benin Kingdom, was a powerful and influential kingdom in West Africa during the medieval and pre-colonial periods.

The Benin people are known for their strong sense of community and their belief in the importance of family and kinship.

One of the most notable aspects of Benin culture is their art, which is known for its intricate and detailed craftsmanship.

The Benin are skilled in a variety of art forms, including woodcarving, bronze casting, and ivory carving.

The Benin are also known for their intricate beadwork, which is used in traditional clothing and jewelry.

The Benin people also have a strong tradition of oral storytelling, with a rich history of folklore and legends passed down through the generations.

Music and dance are also an important part of Benin culture, with traditional instruments such as the udu drum and the sekere gourd being used in traditional music and dance performances.

The Benin people also have a deep respect for their ancestors and follow traditional religious practices.

The Benin believe in a pantheon of gods and goddesses, and the role of traditional priests, known as the Ezen, is central to Benin religious practice.

In terms of social customs, the Benin place a strong emphasis on respect for authority and hierarchy.

Age and status are highly respected within Benin society, and there is a strong tradition of deference to elders and those in positions of authority.

Overall, the culture of the Benin people is rich and diverse, with a strong emphasis on tradition, community, and the importance of family and kinship.

THE ROLE OF THE BENIN PEOPLE IN SHAPING THE BENIN CULTURE

The Benin people have played a significant role in shaping the culture of the Kingdom of Benin, which is located in present-day Nigeria.

The Benin Kingdom was a highly centralized state that was ruled by an oba (king) and a council of chiefs.

The oba was considered to be the divine ruler of the kingdom and was responsible for maintaining order and upholding the traditional laws and customs of the Benin people.

The Benin people have a rich cultural heritage that is reflected in their art, music, dance, and other cultural practices.

The Benin Kingdom was known for its bronze and brass sculpture, which were used to create elaborate works of art that depicted the oba, other members of the royal court, and important historical events. These sculptures were highly prized and were often used as diplomatic gifts.

The Benin people also had a strong oral tradition that was used to preserve their history and cultural practices.

Storytellers, known as "griots," played a central role in this tradition, as they were responsible for passing down the stories and legends of the Benin people from generation to generation.

In addition to their artistic and cultural achievements, the Benin people have also made important contributions to the political and economic development of the region.

The Kingdom of Benin was a major regional power in West Africa, and its political and economic influence extended beyond its borders.

The Benin people played a key role in the development of trade networks in the region, and their expertise in agriculture, metalworking, and other crafts made them an important economic force in the region.

Overall, the Benin people have had a significant impact on the culture and development of the Kingdom of Benin and the region as a whole.

Their rich cultural heritage, artistic achievements, and economic contributions have shaped the character and identity of the Benin people and continue to be an important part of their culture today.

THE BENIN LANGUAGE

The Benin language, also known as Edo, is a language spoken in the Kingdom of Benin, which is located in present-day Nigeria.

It is a member of the Edo language group and is closely related to other languages spoken in the region, such as Esan and Etsako.

Edo is the primary language spoken in the Kingdom of Benin and is used in a variety of contexts, including everyday communication, education, and the media.

It is also spoken by a large number of people in the surrounding region and has a significant presence in the urban areas of Nigeria.

The Benin language has a rich history that is closely tied to the culture and traditions of the Benin people. It has a complex grammar and a large vocabulary, and it is written in a modified version of the Latin alphabet.

The Benin language has a number of dialects that are spoken in different parts of the Kingdom of Benin, and these dialects can vary significantly in terms of pronunciation, vocabulary, and grammar.

In addition to its use in everyday communication, the Benin language has also played a significant role in the cultural and artistic traditions of the Benin people.

It has a rich oral tradition that includes stories, legends, and other forms of oral literature, and it has been used as a medium for transferring traditions and information from one generation to the next.

Overall, the Benin language is an important part of the culture and identity of the Benin people and continues to be an integral part of life in the Kingdom of Benin.

NAMES OF OGISOS

1. Igodo
2. Ere
3. Orire
4. Odia
5. Ighido
6. Evbobo
7. Ogbeide
8. Emehen
9. Akhuankhuan
10. Ekpigho
11. Efeseke
12. Irudia
13. Etebowe
14. Odion
15. Imarhan
16. Orria
17. Emose (female)
18. Orrorro (female)

19. Irrebo
20. Ogbomo
21. Agbonzeke
22. Ediae
23. Oriagba
24. Odoligie
25. Uwa
26. Eheneden
27. Ohuede
28. Oduwa
29. Obioye
30. Arigho
31. Owodo
32. Evian (administrator)
33. Irebor Ogiemwen (administrator)

LIST OF BENIN OBAS

Eweka I (1180–1246)
   Uwuakhuahen (1246–1250)
   Henmihen (1250–1260)
Ewedo (1260–1274)
Oguola (1274–1287)
Edoni (1287–1292)
Akang (1292–1296)
Udagbedo (1296–1329)
Ohen (1329–1366)
Egbeka (1366–1397)
Orobiru (1397–1434)
Uwaifiokun (1434–1440)
Ewuare I (1440–1473)
Ezoti (1473–1474)
Olua (1475–1480)
Ozolua (1480–1504)
Esigie (1504–1547)
Orhogbua (1547–1580)
Ehengbuda (1580–1602)

Ohuan (1602–1656)
Ohenzae (1656-1675)
Akenkpaye (1675–1684)
Akengbedo (1684–1689)
Ore-Oghene (1689–1701)
Ewuakpe (1701–1712)
Ozuere (1712–1713)
Akenzua I (1713–1740)
Eresoyen (1740–1750)
Akengbuda (1750–1804)
Obanosa (1804–1816)
Ogbebo (1816)
Osemwende (1816–1848)
Adolo (1848–1888)
Ovonramwen Nogbaisi (1888–1914) (he was exiled to Calabar in 1897 by the British)
Eweka II (1914–1933)
Akenzua II (1933–1978)
Erediauwa (1979–2016)
Ewuare II (2016–present)

BENIN TRADITIONAL RELIGION

The traditional religion of the Benin people, also known as Edo or Bini, is based on the belief in a supreme being called Osanobua.

The Benin people also believe in a pantheon of deities, known as the orisha, who are responsible for various aspects of life and the natural world.

One of the most important orisha is Eshu, the god of mischief and the messenger of the gods. Other important deities include Olokun, the god of the sea; Ogun, the god of iron and war; and Osun, the goddess of fertility and love.

The traditional religion of the Benin people is polytheistic and includes the worship of ancestors and the use of divination to communicate with the gods.

Many Benin people also practice ancestor veneration, in which they honor their deceased ancestors and ask for their guidance and protection.

In the traditional Benin religion, rituals and ceremonies play a central role. These ceremonies often involve the use of music, dance, and offerings of food and other materials to the gods.

The traditional Benin religion is also closely tied to the arts, with many rituals and ceremonies involving the creation of elaborate masks and sculptures.

Overall, the traditional religion of the Benin people is a complex and multifaceted belief system that is deeply ingrained in the culture and history of the Benin people.

HOLY ARUOSA (THE BENIN CHURCH)

The Holy Aruosa Cathedral is a cathedral that was established in 1517 and is situated in Akpakpava in Benin City, Edo, Nigeria.

Portuguese missionaries and Oba Esigie, the son of Queen Idia, established it.

The church of the Oba of Benin and the senior Binis is the name given to it frequently (people of Benin).

It is one of Nigeria's oldest churches, dating back to the arrival of the Portuguese.

Holy Aruosa Catheral has a sacred book, just like every other Abrahamic religion, and it is referred to as the Book of Holy Aruosa.

The wise men who wrote it used the dictum, teachings, and proverbs of the former Benin kingdom.

THE BENIN TRADITIONAL FASHION

The traditional fashion of the Benin people, also known as the Edo or Bini, is an integral part of the culture and history of this West African nation.

Benin's traditional fashion is characterized by a rich and diverse array of textiles, patterns, and styles that reflect the country's rich cultural heritage.

One of the most distinctive features of Benin's traditional fashion is the use of vibrant colors and intricate patterns.

Many traditional Benin garments are made from hand-woven fabrics that are decorated with elaborate designs and motifs, such as geometric patterns, animals, and abstract shapes.

These patterns and motifs often hold cultural and symbolic significance, and are believed to bring good luck, ward off evil spirits, and protect the wearer from harm.

In addition to clothing, traditional Benin fashion also includes a range of accessories such as jewelry, hats, shoes, and bags. These accessories are often made from materials such as leather, beads, shells, and feathers, and are adorned with intricate patterns and designs.

Overall, the traditional fashion of the Benin people is a vibrant and expressive reflection of the country's rich cultural heritage and artistic traditions.

It continues to be an important aspect of Benin's cultural identity and is celebrated and preserved by the people of Benin to this day.

THE BENIN TRADITIONAL FOOD

Benin cuisine is the traditional cuisine of the Benin people, who are native to the Edo state of Nigeria.

The cuisine is known for its use of spices and flavorful ingredients, and it is often considered to be one of the most flavorful and aromatic cuisines in West Africa.

One of the most popular dishes in Benin cuisine is "Eba," which is made from cassava flour that is mixed with water to form a dough-like consistency.

The dough is then shaped into small balls and boiled in a flavorful broth or sauce. "Eba" is usually served with soup or stew, and it is a staple food in Benin households.

Another popular dish in Benin cuisine is "EMA," which is made from POUNDED yam that is mixed with little water to form a dough-like consistency. The dough is then shaped into balls. "EMA" is also typically served with different kinds of soup, and it is a popular food among the Benin people.

In Bini, you will find soups like:

OGBOLO
OGI
ORIWO
OWHO
EHIURBO
and many more

Benin cuisine is traditionally served with a variety of side dishes, such as plantains, beans, rice, and vegetables. It is typically eaten with the hands, and it is considered a social activity to share food with others in the community.

BENIN ARTS AND CRAFTS

The Benin people of Edo state in Nigeria are known for their artistic and craft-making traditions. Some popular arts and crafts produced by the Benin include:

Benin Bronzes: These are a series of bronze and brass plaques and sculptures created by the Benin people in the Kingdom of Benin. They are considered some of the best examples of African art and are known for their intricate details and craftsmanship.

Beadwork: The Benin are known for their intricate beadwork, which is used to create a variety of decorative items such as jewelry, clothing, and ceremonial objects.

Woodcarving: The Benin are skilled woodcarvers and create a variety of objects such as masks, figures, and furniture using traditional techniques.

Textile arts: The Benin are skilled weavers and produce a variety of textiles using traditional techniques such as hand-loom weaving and tie-dyeing.

Pottery: The Benin produce a variety of pottery, including decorative pots and bowls, using traditional techniques.

Music and dance: The Benin have a rich musical and dance tradition, with a variety of instruments and dance styles.

THE ROLE OF ARTS IN THE BENIN CULTURE

Art plays a significant role in Benin culture, serving as a means of communication, expression, and cultural preservation.

The Benin people have a long tradition of creating a variety of arts, including sculpture, beadwork, woodcarving, textile arts, pottery, and music and dance. These arts are often used to tell stories, convey cultural values, and celebrate important events and ceremonies.

The Benin people are known for their bronze and brass sculpture, which is considered some of the best examples of African art.

The Benin Bronzes, a series of bronze and brass plaques and sculptures created by the Benin people in the Kingdom of Benin, are known for their intricate details and craftsmanship.

These bronzes were originally used to decorate the palace of the Oba (king) of Benin, and depicted a variety of subjects including historical events, animals, and everyday life.

THE ROLE OF ARTS IN THE BENIN CULTURE

Beadwork is another important art form in Benin culture, and is used to create a variety of decorative items such as jewelry, clothing, and ceremonial objects.

Beadwork is often used to convey cultural values and traditions, and is an important part of Benin ceremonies and rituals.

Music and dance are also important components of Benin culture, and play a central role in ceremonies and celebrations.

The Benin have a rich musical tradition, with a variety of instruments including drums, xylophones, and flutes.

FESTIVALS AND CELEBRATIONS OF THE BENIN PEOPLE

The Benin people of Edo state in Nigeria have a variety of festivals and celebrations throughout the year. Some popular festivals and celebrations include:

Igue Festival: This is a major festival that takes place in December and lasts for a week. It is a time of prayer, thanksgiving, and cleansing, and involves a variety of ceremonies and rituals.

Ovu Festival: This festival is held in honor of the god Ovu, and involves a series of ceremonies and rituals, including the sacrifice of animals and the offering of food and drink to the gods.

Ugie-Ewere Festival: This festival is held to honor the god Ewere, and involves a series of ceremonies and rituals, including the sacrifice of animals and the offering of food and drink to the gods.

Ugie-Iyanmwen Festival: This festival is held to honor the god Iyanmwen, and involves a series of ceremonies and rituals, including the sacrifice of animals and the offering of food and drink to the gods.

Igue-Iworho Festival: This festival is held to honor the god Iworho, and involves a series of ceremonies and rituals, including the sacrifice of animals and the offering of food and drink to the gods.

Igue-Iye Festival: This festival is held to honor the god Iye, and involves a series of ceremonies and rituals, including the sacrifice of animals and the offering of food and drink to the gods.

THE TRADITIONAL MARRIAGE CEREMONY OF THE BENIN PEOPLE

The traditional marriage of the Benin people of Edo state, Nigeria is a significant cultural and social event that involves a series of complex rituals and ceremonies.

The process of getting married in the Benin culture starts with the man requesting the hand of the woman in marriage from her family.

If the woman's family agrees to the proposal, the man is expected to pay a bride price, which is a negotiated sum of money and other gifts that are presented to the woman's family as a symbol of the man's commitment and appreciation for their daughter.

The bride price is usually paid in installments, with the final payment made on the day of the wedding.

The traditional Benin wedding ceremony is a grand and elaborate affair that is attended by friends, family, and members of the community.

The couple is traditionally dressed in their traditional wedding attire, and the ceremony is officiated by a traditional marriage counselor.

After the wedding ceremony, the couple is expected to move in with the husband's family and live in the same compound with them.

In the Benin culture, the role of the wife is to support her husband, bear children, and manage the household.

The husband is expected to provide for the family and make all major decisions for the household.

Overall, the traditional marriage of the Benin people is a deeply cultural and significant event that is an important part of their society and way of life.

THE TRADITIONAL BURIAL CEREMONY OF THE BENIN PEOPLE

The traditional burial ceremony of the Benin people of Edo state, Nigeria is a significant cultural and social event that is marked by a series of complex rituals and ceremonies.

Upon the death of a member of the Benin community, the body is usually washed and prepared for burial by the family members.

The body is then placed in a coffin and taken to the home of the deceased, where it is displayed for friends, family, and community members to pay their respects.

The traditional burial ceremony of the Benin people involves a series of rituals and ceremonies that are meant to honor and celebrate the life of the deceased. These rituals may include the "Ighele" ceremony, which involves the presentation of food and gifts to the deceased's family, and the "Igue" ceremony, which involves the chanting of traditional prayers and songs to honor the deceased.

The traditional burial ceremony of the Benin people also involves the

"Ivie-Omo" ceremony, which involves the presentation of the deceased's possessions to their children. This ceremony is meant to symbolize the passing on of the deceased's legacy to the next generation.

After the burial ceremony, the family of the deceased usually holds a reception for friends, family, and community members. This reception may include the serving of traditional foods and drinks, as well as the singing of traditional songs and the telling of stories about the deceased.

Overall, the traditional burial ceremony of the Benin people is a deeply cultural and significant event that is an important part of their society and way of life.

It is a time for the community to come together and honor the life of the deceased, as well as to provide support and comfort to the bereaved family.

SOME TOURIST SITES IN BENIN

Benin City, the capital of Edo state in Nigeria, is home to a number of tourist sites that are popular with both local and international visitors.

Some of the top tourist sites in Benin City include:

Benin Moat: This is a series of defensive walls that were built around the city of Benin in the 14th and 15th centuries. The moat is a UNESCO World Heritage Site and is known for its impressive size and well-preserved condition.

Oba's Palace: This is the traditional palace of the Oba, or king, of Benin. The palace is a stunning example of traditional Benin architecture and is home to a number of museums and art galleries.

National Museum of Benin: This museum is located in the Oba's Palace and is home to a collection of artifacts and historical items that tell the story of the Benin Kingdom.

Emotan Statue: This statue is located in the center of Benin City and is dedicated to Emotan, a legendary figure who is believed to have played a key role in the founding of the city.

Benin Golf Course: This is a popular destination for golf enthusiasts and is known for its well-maintained course and beautiful surroundings.

Overall, Benin City is a city rich in history and culture and offers a wide range of tourist attractions for visitors to enjoy.

SITE AND SOUNDS OF THE BENIN PEOPLE

The site and sounds of the Benin people of Edo state, Nigeria are a reflection of the rich cultural heritage of this community.

One of the most iconic sites in Benin City is the Benin Moat, a series of defensive walls that were built around the city in the 14th and 15th centuries. The moat is a UNESCO World Heritage Site and is known for its impressive size and well-preserved condition.

Another popular site in Benin City is the Oba's Palace, the traditional palace of the Oba, or king, of Benin. The palace is a stunning example of traditional Benin architecture and is home to a number of museums and art galleries.

The sounds of Benin City are just as vibrant and diverse as its sites. The city is home to a number of traditional music and dance styles, such as the "Egungun" dance, which is performed during the annual Egungun Festival, and the "Gelede" dance, which is performed to honor the spirits of the ancestors.

The Benin people are also known for their traditional art, which includes sculptures, bronze castings, and other crafts. The city is home to a number of artisan markets where visitors can purchase traditional Benin crafts and other souvenirs.

Overall, the site and sounds of the Benin people of Edo state offer a glimpse into the rich cultural traditions of this community and are a must-see for anyone visiting the area.

CONCLUSION

In conclusion, the Benin people are a diverse and vibrant culture with a rich history and traditions.

From the stunning artwork and intricate bronze sculptures that have made them famous, to the colorful and lively festivals that celebrate their heritage, the Benin people are truly a sight to behold.

Whether through their music, dance, or art, the Benin people are a testament to the resilience and beauty of the human spirit.

It is this spirit that has allowed them to thrive and preserve their culture for centuries, and it is this spirit that will continue to inspire future generations.

Made in United States
Orlando, FL
06 September 2024